The Little Book of Light and Shadow

Investigating light and shadow in the Foundation Stage

Written by
Linda Thornton and Pat Brunton
Edited by Sally Featherstone
Illustrations by Kerry Ingham

D1637666

LITTLE BOOKS WITH **BIG** IDEAS

This edition published 2013 by Featherstone, an imprint of Bloomsbury Publishing Plc
First published 2003 by A&C Black, an imprint of Bloomsbury Publishing Plc
50 Bedford Square, London WC1B 3DP
www.bloomsbury.com

ISBN 978-1-4729-0654-0

© Featherstone Education Ltd, 2003
Text © Linda Thornton & Pat Brunton, 2003
Series Editor, Sally Featherstone

A CIP record for this publication is available from the British Library.

Printed in Great Britain by Latimer Trend & Company Limited.

This book is produced using paper that is made from wood grown in
managed, sustainable forests. It is natural, renewable and recyclable.

The logging and manufacturing processes conform to the environmental
regulations of the country of origin.

1 3 5 7 9 10 8 6 4 2

**To see our full range of titles
visit www.bloomsbury.com**

Contents

Focus of the page	pages

Introduction

This book is one of the titles in a series of Little Books, which explore aspects of practice within the Early Years Foundation Stage in England. The books are also suitable for practitioners working with the early years curriculum in Wales, Northern Ireland and Scotland, and in any early years setting catering for young children.

Across the series you will find titles appropriate to each aspect of the curriculum for children from two to five years, giving practitioners a wealth of ideas for engaging activities, interesting resources and stimulating environments to enrich their work across the early years curriculum. Outdoor play should be a daily activity, and free access to an outdoor area is an ideal we should all work towards.

Each title also has information linking the activity pages to the statutory early years curriculum for England. This title has been updated to include the revised Early Learning Goals published by the Department for Education in March 2012. The full set of 19 goals is included in the introduction to each book, and the activity pages will refer you to the relevant statements to which each activity contributes.

For the purposes of observation and assessment of the children's work in each activity, we recommend that practitioners should use each of the 'revised statements' as a whole, resisting any impulse to separate the elements of each one into short phrases.

The key goals for this title are highlighted in blue, although other goals may be included on some pages.

PRIME AREAS

Communication and language

(1) **Listening and attention:** children listen attentively in a range of situations. They listen to stories, accurately anticipating key events and respond to what they hear with relevant comments, questions or actions. They give their attention to what others say and respond appropriately, while engaged in another activity.

(2) **Understanding:** children follow instructions involving several ideas or actions. They answer 'how' and 'why' questions about their experiences and in response to stories or events.

(3) **Speaking:** children express themselves effectively, showing awareness of listeners' needs. They use past, present and future forms accurately when talking about events that have happened or are to happen in the future. They develop their own narratives and explanations by connecting ideas or events.

Physical development

(1) **Moving and handling:** children show good control and co-ordination in large and small movements. They move confidently in a range of ways, safely negotiating space. They handle equipment and tools effectively, including pencils for writing.

(2) Health and self-care: children know the importance for good health of physical exercise, and a healthy diet, and talk about ways to keep healthy and safe. They manage their own basic hygiene and personal needs successfully, including dressing and going to the toilet independently.

Personal, social and emotional development

(1) Self-confidence and self-awareness: children are confident to try new activities, and say why they like some activities more than others. They are confident to speak in a familiar group, will talk about their ideas, and will choose the resources they need for their chosen activities. They say when they do or don't need help.

(2) Managing feelings and behaviour: children talk about how they and others show feelings, talk about their own and others' behaviour, and its consequences, and know that some behaviour is unacceptable. They work as part of a group or class, and understand and follow the rules. They adjust their behaviour to different situations, and take changes of routine in their stride.

(3) Making relationships: children play co-operatively, taking turns with others. They take account of one another's ideas about how to organise their activity. They show sensitivity to others' needs and feelings, and form positive relationships with adults and other children.

SPECIFIC AREAS

Literacy

(1) Reading: children read and understand simple sentences. They use phonic knowledge to decode regular words and read them aloud accurately. They also read some common irregular words. They demonstrate understanding when talking with others about what they have read.

(2) Writing: children use their phonic knowledge to write words in ways which match their spoken sounds. They also write some irregular common words. They write simple sentences which can be read by themselves and others. Some words are spelt correctly and others are phonetically plausible.

Mathematics

(1) Numbers: children count reliably with numbers from 1 to 20, place them in order and say which number is one more or one less than a given number. Using quantities and objects, they add and subtract two single-digit numbers and count on or back to find the answer. They solve problems, including doubling, halving and sharing.

(2) Shape, space and measures: children use everyday language to talk about size, weight, capacity, position, distance, time and money to compare quantities and objects and to solve problems. They recognise, create and describe patterns. They explore characteristics of everyday objects and shapes and use mathematical language to describe them.

Understanding the world

(1) People and communities: children talk about past and present events in their own lives and in the lives of family members. They know that other children don't always enjoy the same things, and are sensitive to this. They know about similarities and differences between themselves and others, and among families, communities and traditions.

(2) The world: children know about similarities and differences in relation to places, objects, materials and living things. They talk about the features of their own immediate environment and how environments might vary from one another. They make observations of animals and plants and explain why some things occur, and talk about changes.

(3) Technology: children recognise that a range of technology is used in places such as homes and schools. They select and use technology for particular purposes.

Expressive arts and design

(1) Exploring and using media and materials: children sing songs, make music and dance, and experiment with ways of changing them. They safely use and explore a variety of materials, tools and techniques, experimenting with colour, design, texture, form and function.

(2) Being imaginative: children use what they have learnt about media and materials in original ways, thinking about uses and purposes. They represent their own ideas, thoughts and feelings through design and technology, art, music, dance, role-play and stories.

Light

Light is magical – and so is darkness.

The magic of light is the touch on clouds of the rising or setting sun; the crisp, clear brightness of a sunny day; the excitement of lights at Christmas or Diwali; or the comforting flicker of firelight.

The magic of darkness is seeing stars against the black velvet of a night sky; the anticipation as lights dim in a theatre or cinema; or the imaginary worlds children make when they put their heads under the bedclothes to shut out the light.

But darkness also has a scary side, because by depriving us of our major sense it makes us feel vulnerable and insecure. Many children (and some adults!) are not only afraid in the dark, but are afraid of the dark. It's not for nothing that we use the term 'being in the dark' to cover all sorts of situations where we feel lacking in knowledge, poorly informed and disadvantaged.

The phenomena of light and its absence have fascinated mankind since time began. Even 100 years ago, children would have had a very different experience of light and dark. Nowadays we take for granted the easy control of light, but children then would have known more darkness and would have experienced being in the dark more often.

... and dark

For them, darkness would have been commonplace – and therefore light would probably have been even more dramatic and welcome. Few people in the northern hemisphere today experience the contrast between light and dark with such regular intensity.

Nowadays many children never experience true darkness at all. 'Light pollution' – the spillage of light from buildings and streets, destroys the impact of the dark. Lit streets are safer, without a doubt, and lights in and around buildings add immeasurably to the richness of our daily lives. But we pay a price for these things. Urban children have few opportunities to see the stars in their full glory, or to develop that experience of darkness which helps them to understand why light is such an important element in our language and literature, and in many of our major religious and secular festivals.

This book has a scientific focus, which is investigating and explaining light and shadow. However, true science extends beyond recording and explanation. We hope you will also take on board a broader aim of the book, which is to build on the activities we present here to help children to know the wonder of light, and to feel the drama of darkness.

Setting the scene

Supporting children's learning

Children's interest in the world around them, and their desire to investigate, will vary. Some will be naturally curious and will have been encouraged to be so from a very early age. Others may need more support and to be given 'permission to take risks' in a secure and safe environment.

Some children will enjoy exploring and investigating on their own; others will prefer to be with a friend, an adult, or part of a group. 'Shadows on the wall' could be investigated by a child playing alone, or as part of a small group of 3 or 4 children. 'Imaginary worlds' and 'Whose shadow is it?' require cooperation by a group of children.

As children become involved in their investigations, they will start to be absorbed and concentrate for long periods of time. Some explorations which arise from the ideas in this book may continue for days, weeks or even months. Alternatively children may wish to revisit an activity periodically to develop their ideas further.

Many children in the Foundation Stage have reached a point where they enjoy working independently but still appreciate a little adult help on occasion. This is often a difficult situation to manage. It requires very 'active listening' on the part of the practitioner to judge the moment for appropriate intervention in children's discoveries. This means standing back and watching, listening to children's conversations (with others or themselves!) and recognising cues which invite your participation. It is not always easy – resist the urge to interfere.

Placing conversations at the centre of your work with children celebrates their natural curiosity and wonder about the world and how it works.

Careful thinking lies behind children's ideas – their theories may not always be based on scientific reasoning but they are valuable as they make sense to the children at the time. It is important that you trust the children to come up with good ideas, and that you take them seriously.

Talking with children about their ideas and asking them questions helps to develop creative and critical thinking skills. Asking good questions needs thought, organisation, planning and lots of practice.

Good questions are often open ended and invite children to express their thoughts and ideas. For example:

▶ 'Do you think everything has a shadow?'

▶ 'How do you think shadows are made?'

Remember you are not looking for the 'right' answer. Instead, by emphasising the 'you' in these questions, you are giving a clear message that everyone's ideas and opinions are important.

Good questions may pose problems which then invite further investigation and exploration. For example:

▶ 'Who do you think will have the tallest shadow?'

▶ 'Can you find a way to make the shadows bigger?'

Not every question needs to be open ended. In discussions with a group of children you might include attention focusing questions such as:

▶ 'Have you seen the patterns the projector makes on the wall?'

and measuring and counting questions such as:

▶ 'How many different torches have we collected?'

Good questions involve all children by encouraging then to talk about their experiences. For example:

▶ 'What can you remember about the shadows we made outside?'

▶ 'Do you remember when we lit the candles on the birthday cake?'

Not only is it important that you, as adults, ask good questions; you also need to encourage children to ask questions themselves. You can do this best by:

▶ providing lots of opportunities for children to ask questions

▶ valuing their answers

▶ modelling a questioning mind by thinking out loud – 'I wonder why some shadows are darker than others?

▶ giving children time to think and to respond – don't fill the silences

▶ listening to children's responses before framing the next question.

Knowledge, skills, dispositions and feelings

Knowledge

There will be occasions when the children need to 'borrow' your skills, knowledge and expertise. The investigations in this book are based around a particular scientific concept – light and shadow. To get the most out of the investigation of light and shadow you need to have an understanding of the science and design technology involved so you can help the children to investigate their own ideas. You can find information at the back of the book to help you with this.

Skills

Investigating light and shadow gives opportunities to develop a wide range of important skills. These include:

▶ The social skills of cooperation, negotiation, leadership, following instructions and behaving in a safe manner.

▶ Communication skills including speaking, listening, discussing and recording.

▶ Practical skills including observation, using all the senses, manual dexterity, fine motor control, hand eye coordination and construction.

▶ Reasoning and thinking skills, including questioning, speculating and inferring, problem solving, noticing similarities and differences and reflecting.

Skills improve with practice and children need plenty of opportunities to try out and develop their new skills in as many different ways as possible.

Talking to the children about what they already know provides you with insights into the world they inhabit outside your setting. It gives you the opportunity to value the input and involvement of parents, carers and the child's wider family. You could suggest that the children go on a shadow hunt at home, bring in torches to add to the light display or notice when it gets light in the morning and dark at night. Involving parents in this way will not only help them to be active in their own children's learning but will also enable you to draw on extra resources to benefit all the children in your setting. Perhaps you will discover one of the parents or other family members is an 'expert' on some aspect of light or shadow and would be eager to share this with the children!

Dispositions

To help children to master the range of skills they need, there is a range of behaviours or 'positive dispositions' which you can help to foster. Dispositions are unlikely to be learned from direct instruction. They are far more likely to be learned from the models provided by the significant people in children's lives, both adults and other children. The investigations in this book will help you to encourage:

▶ curiosity

▶ open mindedness

▶ willingness to put forward ideas

▶ critical reflection.

For example, experiencing 'Shadow play' and 'Make it bigger!' will motivate children to become:

▶ confident, independent learners.

Investigating over a longer period of time will encourage:

▶ concentration

▶ perseverance.

Using the overhead projector on a regular basis will give children the opportunity to keep returning to investigations which:

▶ develop their own interests.

As with skills, in order for these dispositions to become embedded children need plenty of opportunities for regular practice.

Feelings

Although you as adults may be very familiar with shadows - big and small - remember that many children will be experiencing this excitement and wonder for the first time. Children invest a great deal of emotion and feeling in the thinking that goes into their ideas and theories. Their comments and observations can be very profound at times and demonstrate deep thinking of a spiritual nature.

Don't forget - contagious enthusiasm is a great learning tool.

How the investigations work

1. Getting started

This section tells you about the resources, space, time and organisation needed before beginning the activity. Examples of resources are given and health and safety considerations are highlighted as safety tips, indicated by an exclamaiton mark.

2. Talking and thinking

This is your opportunity to introduce the investigation, find out what the children already know, think and talk about ideas to explore. You will need to agree who will work together, what size the group will be, which children will work alone and who will investigate what.

3. Exploring

This section shows the steps to follow in carrying out the investigation. It suggests questions you might ask and ways to support the children when they explore. As the children grow in confidence they will increasingly come up with their own ideas to try.

4. Documenting

Here we suggest ways in which you can capture the learning process as children explore and investigate. It includes opportunities for making visual and verbal records of the investigation through the use of photos, tape recordings, and written transcripts of children's conversations and comments.

Let the children take some of the photographs themselves and record their own conversations (dictaphones are easy to use). Allow time for the children to revisit what they have seen and what they have said.

All of us, adults and children, can benefit from the opportunity to revisit a discussion to hear what was said by ourselves as well as others. It helps us to begin to understand how an idea or theory developed.

As practitioners, you will find that spending time reviewing the comments made by children, along with their pictures and photographs, will help you in the completion of the Foundation Stage Profile and in planning effectively for the next stage of their learning.

Ideas are included for interesting ways to display the children's discoveries to share with parents, carers and the local community. The display will provide a starting point for further investigations.

Safety

The investigations in 'The Little Book of Light and Shadow' provide lots of interesting and unusual activities for young children to experience. In your setting you will have a Health and Safety policy which guides your work with children. In addition you will be familiar with your Risk Assessment process which you will complete routinely before introducing any new activity.

Many of the investigations, particularly those on electricity, candles, the dark and 'A shade for Teddy' provide ideal opportunities to focus on different aspects of keeping safe.

Where there are particular safety points to bear in mind we have included at the start of each activity. We repeat them below.

Sun
▶ Never look directly at the sun.
▶ Wear sun protection on sunny days.
▶ If you take mirrors outside be careful that they don't reflect the sun straight into children's eyes.

Candles and fire
▶ Talk to the children about fire safety.
▶ Always supervise burning candles.
▶ Use a baking tray with sand in it to stand a candle before lighting it. If the candle falls over, the sand will put out the flame.

Plants, seeds and soil
▶ Always wash your hands after handling plants, seeds or soil.
▶ Take care to use plants and seeds that are non-poisonous. If in doubt, don't!
▶ Never put seeds in your mouth.

Electricity
▶ Talk to the children about the care that is needed when using mains electricity.
▶ Explain to children that batteries are safe to handle as they are, but are dangerous if damaged or taken to pieces.
▶ Use an overhead projector which does not heat up when left on for long periods.
▶ Position the projector close to the wall socket. Tape down all leads.
▶ Make sure the projector is at the correct height for children to use.
▶ Keep resources well organised and close to the projector.

Handling tools
▶ Make sure children are provided with the appropriate size tools.
▶ Show them how to handle the tools safely, and to use them properly.
▶ Provide safety glasses for any activities which involve drilling or sawing.

Where does light come from?

What you need:

This is a good investigation to do in the winter when the children will be more aware of dark mornings and evenings.

▶ Make a collection of pictures and photographs of day and night scenes.

▶ Gather together suitable materials to make a den outside – sheets, blankets, cardboard or a groundsheet.

▶ Talk to the parents/carers about the investigation and ask them to help by talking to the children about day and night, light and dark. Ask them to take the children outside in the evening or early morning to experience sunrise and sunset.

Do not look directly at the sun.

Making connections

This activity could link with topics on dark and light; times of day; and seasons.

Key words

day	**night**
light	**dark**
morning	**evening**
sunrise	**sunset**
summer	**winter**
sun	**time**

Talking and thinking:

▶ Look at the pictures and photographs with the children.

▶ Talk about the things which happen during the day and the things which happen at night. Listen to their ideas about day and night, light and dark.

Ask: 'Was it light when you got up today?' 'Do you think it will be dark when you go home?'

Exploring:

Go outside at different times of day, as it gets light in the morning, or dark in the afternoon. How easy is it to see things?

Investigate whether it is easier to see things on a bright sunny day, or on a dull day. How easy is it to recognise your friend when it is getting dark?

Make a den outdoors on a sunny day – investigate what is it like inside.

Documenting:

▶ Record or note down children's comments about light and dark and their theories about where light comes from.

▶ Record their feelings about day and night.

▶ Create a display of things that happen during the day, and things that happen at night.

More investigations

Put some small coloured blocks outside and, as it gradually gets light in the morning or dark in the afternoon, let the children investigate how easy it is to spot the blocks and say what colour they are.

Are some colours and shapes easier to see than others?

Who put the light out?

What you need:

This is a good investigation to do in the winter when children will be more aware of darkness and artificial light.

▶ Gather together some pictures of lights and make a starter collection of different light sources – torches, lamps, plug in night lights, fairy lights, rope lights, candles and lanterns. The children will be able to add to this during the investigation.

▶ Find a space in your setting that can be made dark. This could be a den made with blankets and drapes, or a separate area with the lights switched off.

> **Warn the children about the care needed when using mains electricity and candles.**

Making connections

This activity could link with topics on 'Special lights' (p20); 'Whose shadow is it?' (p40); and 'Shadow play' (p50).

Key words

dark	light
bulb	battery
lamp	switch
bright	soft
lantern	candle
torch	spotlight

Talking and thinking:

▶ Talk about different sources of light – electric lights, torches, candles and fire.

▶ Think about things that are hard to do when there is no light.

▶ Discuss with the children their feelings about light and dark.

Ask: 'Do you like bright or soft lights best?' 'How do you feel when the lights are switched off?'

Exploring:

Encourage the children to use different torches to light up their dark space or den.

Are bigger torches always better?

What happens when you use more than one torch?

Investigate with the children the different effects produced by:

▶ spotlights

▶ coloured lights

▶ rope lights

Documenting:

▶ Make a display of the different sources of light you have collected.

▶ Write some of the children's comments on light and investigations with torches.

▶ Add these to the display.

More investigations

Use torches for dramatic effect in a puppet show.

Help the children to change the lighting levels to create different effects during role play. You could install a dimmer switch.*

Use torches as spotlights in small world play situations.

*Must be done by a qualified electrician

Lights outside

What you need:

This is a good investigation for autumn or winter when there will be lots of examples of outside lighting for children to notice.

▶ Provide a range of photographs of lights being used outside – street lights, car headlamps, flood lights, security lights, shop windows, advertising signs, traffic lights.

▶ Gather together a collection of children's coats of different colours, including some with reflective strips, and a fluorescent safety jacket if you can.

▶ Provide a selection of torches.

▶ Make a den inside, or find a dark place where you can test out the different coats to see which ones are easiest to see in the dark.

▶ Enlist the help of parents and carers. Ask them to draw children's attention to outside lights on car journeys, or to take their children out on a light walk.

Making connections

This investigation could follow on from 'Who put the light out?' on p16.

It provides an ideal opportunity to talk about road safety, and the importance of being seen easily at night.

Key words

light	dark
shiny	dull
moon	night
fluorescent	reflect
torch	lamp
safety	beam

Talking and thinking:

▶ Listen to children's ideas and feelings about the dark.

▶ Talk about all the different sorts of lights there are outside. Discuss their ideas on why it might be important to be seen easily at night.

▶ Look at your photograph collection and talk about all the different activities which go on at night.

Ask: 'What would happen if all the lights went out?'

Exploring:

Hang up all the coats in the den or dark area. Are any of them easier to see than others?

Switch on a torch and look at the coats. Which ones are easiest to see?

Take a selection of objects, some shiny and some dull, into the den.

Switch on the torch. Which ones are easiest to see?

Documenting:

▶ Record the children's ideas and feelings about the dark.

▶ Make a display of the children's investigations with torches and different coloured clothing.

▶ Link this with their ideas about why it is important to be seen at night.

(See the end of the book for more resources and contacts.)

More investigations

Go out on a light walk and see how many types of outdoor lights you can find.

Ask the parents/carers to help children experience moonlight and darkness.

If you have a security light, encourage the children to investigate what happens when they stand in different places.

Special lights

What you need:

This is a good investigation for autumn/winter. It links with a number of different festivals and celebrations on the theme of light and is a good opportunity to talk about fire safety.

▶ Make a collection of candles of different sizes, shapes, colours and scents.

▶ Gather together a range of pictures of festivals of light, decorative lights, candles burning, bonfires and fireworks.

▶ **Warn children about fire safety. Always supervise burning candles and never leave children unattended with any sort of flame.**

▶ **Use plasticene or damp sand to hold tall thin candles upright and stand candles in a baking tray of sand to keep them safe if they are accidentally knocked over.**

Making connections

This investigation links with topics on celebrations and festivals; what things are made of; 'Where does light come from?' (p14); and keeping safe.

Key words

candle	light
wax	wick
fire	flame
bonfire	fireworks
safety	danger

Talking and thinking:

▶ Talk with the children about their experiences of light festivals.

▶ Discuss fire safety with them and agree a set of rules for investigating the candles.

Ask: 'Do you remember when we lit the candles on the birthday cake?' 'What do you think happens when we light a candle?' 'Will a candle burn forever?'

Exploring:

Investigate the shape, size, smell, colour of the different candles.

Light a candle and watch carefully as it burns.

What is happening?

What colour is the flame? Is it all the same colour?

What happens to the candle when the flame goes out?

Tell children never to play alone with matches, lighters or lit candles.

Documenting:

▶ Ask the children to draw pictures of a lit candle and to describe what they think is happening. Make a note of these comments.

▶ Display the collection of candles you have made, photographs of a burning candle, the children's ideas about burning, and their fire safety rules. Use this as a focus for a 'Fire Safety Campaign.'

More investigations

Use candles to change the atmosphere in your setting. Make sure you use safe and appropriate candle holders.

Compare different sized candles. How are they different? Which one is the best?

Watch what happens to a candle flame if the wind blows.

Plants and light

What you need:

▶ Take the children on an exploration of the outdoor area of your setting at different times of day.

▶ Draw their attention to the areas that are in the sun and the areas that are in the shade. Note which areas have lots of different plants growing in them, and which have only a few. Look at the different types of plants that grow in sunny and shady areas.

▶ Look out for, and investigate, shady places under bushes and trees – especially conifers.

▶ Ask the children to go on a plant hunt indoors to find out where indoor plants grow well.

▶ Provide: cress seeds; blotting paper/kitchen paper; plastic container; radish seeds; peas or beans; plant trays and pots; potting compost and tools.

Remind the children to wash their hands after this activity.

Making connections

This investigation could follow on from 'On a sunny day' (p34). It links with 'Looking closely' (p26) and 'Make it bigger' (p46). It provides a good opportunity to look at change over time.

Key words

light	dark
water	soil
sunny	shady
seed	grow
flower	plant
change	compost

Talking and thinking:

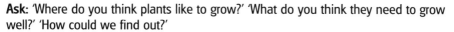

▶ Discuss with the children their ideas about growing plants.

▶ Investigate with them the different types of seeds and talk about the plants they will grow into.

Ask: 'Where do you think plants like to grow?' 'What do you think they need to grow well?' 'How could we find out?'

Exploring:

Grow some cress seeds on paper and investigate what happens if there is no water or no light (put into a sealed box). Look at the seeds every day to note the changes. Encourage the children to draw and describe what they see. Compare their drawings with pictures and photos of plants and seeds.

Grow some radish seeds and then plant them outside, some in a sunny spot and some in a shady spot. Look at them regularly to see which grows best.

Documenting:

▶ Keep a diary with drawings and photographs of the different seedlings as they grow. Include the children's comments and their ideas on where and how plants grow best.

▶ Use the overhead projector to magnify some of the drawings to make drapes and banners.

More investigations

Cover up some grass with a black bin liner – see what happens.

Put a house plant in a dark place for several weeks, and see what happens.

Investigate daisies and Livingstone daisies to see how they react to the sun. The name daisy comes from 'day's eye'. Why might that be?

Use your eyes

What you need:

This investigation is about using our sense of sight as well as all our other senses.

▶ Make a collection of glasses, magnifiers, telescopes and binoculars, bug eye viewers and kaleidoscopes.

▶ Find a selection of photographs of objects taken at unusual angles.

▶ You could take your own pictures of familiar objects in your setting, photographed from unusual angles.

▶ Make a feel box and gather together some interesting objects to put in it.

▶ Provide an audio tape of different sounds for a listening challenge.

▶ Make a collection of different scents and smells – pot pourri, candles, aromatherapy oils and food flavourings.

Making connections

This investigation gives opportunities to develop descriptive language. It helps children to understand how important our senses are, and to be aware of the challenges faced by people with sensory disability.

Key words

eyes	sight
ears	sound
nose	smell
mouth	taste
fingers	touch
hands	feel

Talking and thinking:

▶ Discuss with the children their ideas about their senses and how they use them.

Ask: 'How do we know what is happening outside?' 'Can you hear with your eyes closed?' 'Could you recognise your friend with your eyes shut?' 'What does music taste like?' 'How can we see a long way away?'

Exploring:

Use a feel box to investigate objects by touch alone.

Use the photos of unusual views to match up with the correct objects in the setting.

In pairs, investigate how to find your way around with your eyes closed.

Use magnifiers, and binoculars or telescopes to investigate looking closely, seeing far away or making things easier to see.

Documenting:

▶ Help the children to make their own tape recordings of sounds for others to guess.

▶ Display the 'unusual photograph' collection alongside children's ideas of what they think the objects are.

▶ Set out the feel box and record all the new descriptive words invented by the children.

More investigations

Use a sound tape to investigate how good we are at using our ears.

Explore different smells and scents with your eyes closed.

Which are easiest to recognise? Is it the same for everyone?

Can you see round corners? How could you do this?

Looking closely

What you need:

For this investigation you will need a selection of natural materials – leaves, flowers, feathers, seeds, pine cones, bark, leaf skeletons, shells and stones. Display these attractively and encourage the children to handle them with care. You may like to include some minibeasts which can later be set free again.

▶ For looking closely at pattern and detail the children will need hand held magnifiers and, if possible, a table top version.

▶ To encourage fine drawing, provide a range of drawing material including pencils, fine tip pens and good quality drawing paper.

▶ Set up this investigation in a well lit area in your setting and encourage the children to spend time looking closely and drawing carefully what they see.

This is an ideal investigation to carry out on a light box, as this brings out the fine detail in the objects being investigated.

Making connections

This activity encourages children to concentrate for long periods of time, developing hand-eye coordination and fine motor control. The drawings will provide good examples to use in the 'Megabeasts' overhead projector investigation on page 46 ('Make it bigger!').

Key words

colour	shape
pattern	texture
leaf	flower
seed	shell
bigger	magnifying glass
viewer	bug box

I will need

Talking and thinking:

▶ Talk about the similarities and differences between the materials you have gathered together.

▶ Encourage the children to sort the materials into groups depending on how easy it is to see through them.

Ask: 'Which things go together in a group?' 'Why?' 'Which things are easy to see through?'

Exploring:

Investigate what the world looks like when viewed through different transparent materials.

Try again using a translucent material.

Describe what you see in words and pictures.

Find a range of other transparent, translucent and opaque materials to add to the collection.

Documenting:

▶ Make a display of the different groups of materials accompanied by your transcripts of the comments and observations the children have made on how things look.

▶ Include any new words they have invented to describe their findings.

More investigations

Try looking through transparent coloured materials – coloured acetate or sweet wrappers.

Look through plastic bottles filled with water, dilute orange squash, cold tea, food colouring or cooking oil. Describe how things look.

Seeing clearly

What you need:

Gather together a selection of:

▶ transparent materials which you can see through easily, including clear plastic sheet, plastic bottles, glass containers.

▶ opaque materials you can't see through, including cardboard, wood, metal, stone.

▶ translucent materials that let light pass through, but which you can't see clearly through, such as greaseproof paper, tracing paper and some types of plastic.

Use these as a starting point for discussion with the children.

> **Remind the children never to look directly at the sun, even through coloured plastics or gels.**

Making connections

This investigation links with topics on light and dark and what things are made of. It provides a good opportunity for sorting and classifying materials.

Key words

see	transparent
plastic	metal
wood	stone
clear	translucent
glass	materials
opaque	through

Talking and thinking:

▶ Discuss with the children their ideas about how we see things.

▶ Examine the magnifiers together and find out how the children think they work. Record these ideas.

▶ Play a 'Who can notice?' game.

▶ Talk about the shape, texture, colour and patterns of the natural objects.

▶ Discuss the need to handle objects and live animals with care.

Exploring:

Using the magnifiers, investigate the shape, pattern and structure of one or two different objects.

Make drawings of these and not down any observations of ideas which arise while the drawings are being made.

Try using different drawing materials or types of paper and investigate the different effects produced.

Documenting:

▶ Display the pictures and drawings made by the children alongside photographs of the objects they have been drawing. Accompany this with transcripts of the children's comments and descriptions as they were carrying out the investigation.

▶ At the end of the investigation collect these together to make a permanent record to share with parents and children in the future.

Use a light box to illuminate objects from below and help to focus children's attention.

Try putting some of the children's drawings onto an overhead projector and magnifying them.

How can I make a light work?

What you need:

Understanding how electricity works isn't easy, so this activity may be more appropriate for the older children in your setting. This investigation will help children to develop an understanding of how to make a very simple electrical circuit. It will work best with a small group where children can share their ideas and discoveries. It requires adult involvement.

▶ For the investigation each child will need a rectangular 4.5 volt battery with brass strip (see the picture opposite), connectors and a torch bulb.

▶ **Talk about the difference between mains electricity and batteries.**

▶ **Ensure the children understand that while the equipment you have given them is safe to investigate, plugs, sockets, switches and electric lamps are not. Remember that batteries are safe to handle as they are, but are dangerous if damaged or taken to pieces.**

Making connections

This investigation follows on from 'Who put the light out?' (p14). It will extend children's technical vocabulary and provide them with opportunities to describe exactly how they have done something.

Key words

safety	danger
electricity	energy
lead	clip
torch	battery
bulb	switch
circuit	plug

Talking and thinking:

▶ Talk to the children about battery powered toys and equipment such as torches, radios and personal stereos.

▶ Talk about the battery being a source of stored electrical energy.

▶ Look at the bulb and talk about what it is made of.

Ask: 'What do you think batteries are for?' 'Do you think you could make the bulb light up?'

Exploring:

Using just the bulb and the battery, ask the children if they can find a way to make the bulb light up. (This may take some time, but resist the temptation to show them what to do!)

When the first child is successful ask them to explain exactly how they did it. There will then be great excitement as all the children in the group then light up their bulbs.

Documenting:

▶ Make drawings, and take photographs of the circuit.

▶ Collect the children's drawings of the battery and the bulb and of their completed electrical circuits. Display these with their ideas on how they think the different components work.

▶ Take photographs of the circuit building activity and the successful outcomes and display these alongside a model of a circuit.

More investigations

Look closely at the light bulb through a magnifier.

Can you see the thin wire inside the bulb?

Investigate how to light up a bulb away from the battery – you will need leads and crocodile clips for this (see 'Fairy lights', p32).

READY

4.5 Volt

31

Fairy lights

What you need:

I will need

This investigation builds on the children's discoveries about how a circuit works from 'How can I make a light work?' (p30). As before, it may be more appropriate for older children.

You will need:

▶ a battery for each child

▶ a number of bulbs

▶ bulb holders

▶ leads with crocodile clips attached. This is an ideal investigation to carry out on a light box, as this brings out the fine detail in the objects being investigated.

Provide multiple sets of components so the children can investigate lots of different ways of making the lights work. Work with a small group at a time and let the children choose what they want to use.

Encourage cooperation, teamwork and sharing of ideas.

Hang up a set of fairy lights for children to look at.

Making connections

This investigation follows on directly from 'How can I make a light work?' (p30). It will link with topics on light and dark; Christmas; Diwali and other festivals of light.

Key words

bright	dim
twinkle	shine
bulb	buzzer
holder	clip
circuit	lead

Talking and thinking:

▶ Reflect on children's ideas and understanding of circuits from previous investigations.

▶ Talk about the fairy lights and look at the way the lights follow on from one another in the string.

▶ Discuss with the children how think they might be able to link their components together to make more than one bulb light up.

Exploring:

Using the batteries, leads and bulbs, let the children work individually or in pairs and see if they can make more than one bulb light up at the same time.

Investigate how many different ways there are to do this.

Documenting:

▶ Record the children's comments as they are carrying out this investigation – use a battery powered tape recorder or memo taker!

▶ Ask the children to make drawings of the different circuits they have created.

▶ Take photographs to display alongside the pictures and comments.

More investigations

How many bulbs can you put into a single circuit?

How brightly do the lights shine?

Make 'musical fairy lights' by adding a buzzer into your circuit!

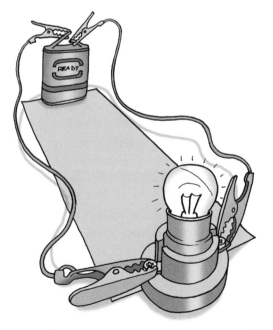

On a sunny day

What you need:

▶ Choose a sunny day to explore shadows outside. (Remember this could be in the winter as well as in the summer.)

▶ Go out on a shadow hunt in the grounds of your setting, or in the local park.

▶ Look all around you for shadows of different shapes and sizes.

▶ Take paper and crayons and a camera with you so that you and the children can record your investigations.

▶ **When it is very hot, remember to protect the children from the sun.**

▶ **Remind the children never to look directly at the sun.**

Making connections

This activity could link with topics on weather; light; and myself.

Key words

tallest	shortest
biggest	smallest
still	move
same	different
shape	outline
shadow	compare

Talking and thinking:

▶ Discuss with the children the shadows they can see.

▶ Ask the children to describe the shadows.

Ask: 'Where can you see shadows?' 'Do you think everything has a shadow?' 'Who do you think will have the tallest shadow?'

Exploring:

On the shadow hunt, look for the biggest and the smallest shadows.

Encourage the children to compare their own shadows with those of their friends.

Ask them to help one another to draw round their shadows.

Take the 'shadows' back inside and compare their sizes and shapes.

Ask: 'How do you think shadows are made?'

Documenting:

▶ Take photographs of the shadows that you find outside. Use them later to talk about the shadows and their shapes.

▶ Record what the children say as they recall their shadow hunt and talk about how shadows are made.

▶ Make a display of the photographs and the children's comments.

More investigations

Use the display to remind the children about their 'shadow ideas'.

Go outside at different times of the day and investigate with the children how shadows change in shape and size.

Find shadows that stay still and shadows that move.

Watching shadows move

What you need:

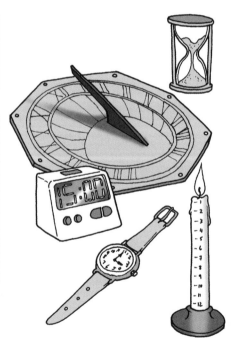

▶ Make a collection of things that measure time. You could include a clock, a watch, a digital timer, a sand timer, a cooking timer, a candle clock and a sundial. Include photographs and pictures, and ask families to help.

▶ Spend some time talking with the children about the many different ways in which time is measured.

▶ Talk about times of the day and about hours and minutes. Play 'What's the time, Mr Wolf?'

▶ Watch the weather forecast and choose a sunny day to investigate measuring time using a shadow clock. Hang up a set of fairy lights for children to look at.

You will also need a marker stick or a cone and some string or chalk for this investigation.

Making connections

This investigation follows on from 'On a sunny day' (p34). It links with topics on time; seasons; and change.

Key words

time	day
watch	sundial
sun	candle
hour	minute
cone	chalk
clock	bracket

Talking and thinking:

▶ Discuss the children's 'shadow theories'. Build on what they already know about shadows changing size and shape over time.

▶ Show the children a sundial and ask them what they think it is. Some will already have seen a sundial and may have ideas about how it works.

Ask the children which times of the day are most important to them.

Exploring:

Take the sundial outside and investigate what happens when it is placed in a sunny spot.

As a group, set up an investigation to measure time using shadows, using a stick in soft earth or in a pot, or a cone on a hard surface.

Agree the special times of the day you will look at the stick (or cone) to see what has happened to the shadow.

Documenting:

▶ At the children's special times, mark the shadow's position with a chalk mark or string.

▶ Give the children a camera to record the changes at different times of the day.

▶ Display the pictures with photographs of special times of the day.

More investigations

With the children, make a wall sundial by fixing a hanging basket bracket where the sun will shine on it. Mark the shadow lines on the wall.

Investigate which parts of the outdoor area are in the shade at different times of the day, and why.

Can only the sun make shadows?

What you need:

You can do this investigation easily, even with the youngest children.

▶ Involve the children in creating a dark place in your setting.
You could:

▷ draw the blinds or curtains

▷ dim the lights

▷ create a cave under a table or using a large box

▷ use a clothes horse and blankets to make a tent.

▶ Gather together a collection of objects that will make interesting shadows – some large and some small.

▶ Include objects made of different materials, including some transparent and translucent things.

▶ Provide a selection of torches of different sizes. You will also need a marker stick or a cone and some string or chalk for this investigation.

> ## Making connections
> This activity will link with topics on light and dark and what are things made of.

Key words

light	shadow
torch	bulb
wood	plastic
dark	shade
switch	material
metal	glass

Talking and thinking:

▶ Talk about what you need to make a shadow – a solid object and a light source.

▶ Think about the sorts of shadows different objects will make.

▶ Encourage the children to talk about what they already know about shadows. Revisit their 'shadow theories' from 'Watching shadows move', pages 36-7.

Ask: 'Can you remember when...?'

Exploring:

In groups of two or three, let the children investigate making shadows using the torches and objects they have chosen. Working in groups will develop cooperation and discussion.

Encourage them to explore ways of changing the shape and size of their shadow patterns. They may need help in holding the torch and moving it backwards and forwards.

Documenting:

▶ Use a tape recorder to capture what the children say as they investigate their shadow patterns. This will allow them to share their discoveries in a larger group.

▶ Provide opportunities for children to make pictures of the shadows they have observed.

More investigations

Investigate which objects make the most interesting shadows.

Investigate the different materials the objects are made from.

Investigate which torch makes the best shadows.

Ask: 'Can you switch a shadow off?'

Whose shadow is it?

What you need:

▶ Secretly put together a collection of everyday objects which you think will make interesting shadows. You might choose a whisk, a bunch of keys, a fork, a pair of scissors or a teapot.

▶ Choose a dark place in your setting - draw the blinds, or use screens or drapes to block out the light.

▶ You need a strong torch, a small table or stool, and a space for the children to sit facing a blank part of the wall.

▶ One person acts as the 'shadow maker' and the others have to guess what is making the shadow. The shadow maker chooses an object and places it on the table or stool.

▶ Then they switch the torch on so the shadow is thrown on to the wall in front of the children.

Making connections

This investigation links with topics on light and dark; day and night; and using our senses.

Key words

whisk	shadow
scissors	torch
bunch	object
fork	behind
keys	in front
teapot	silhouette

Talking and thinking:

▶ Tell the children that you are going to play a game called 'Whose shadow is it?'

▶ To play the game they have to follow the instructions carefully. The game will only work if they sit facing the wall and don't turn round when the torch comes on.

▶ Explain that they will each be able to have a turn at being the 'shadow maker'.

Exploring:

Ask the children to sit facing the wall.

Switch on the torch and turn out the lights.

Stand behind the children and shine the torch on the wall.

Hold an object in front of the torch so that a shadow falls on the wall.

Ask the children 'What do you think this is?', ' How do you know?'

Let the children take turns in being the shadow maker.

Documenting:

▶ Ask another adult to record the ideas individual children have about what the shadows are.

▶ Make a book with the shadow outlines and the comments children have made.

▶ Use this as starting point to develop their creative explorations.

More investigations

Try making shadow shapes with your hands – birds, insects, animals and monsters!

Try making shadow portraits or silhouettes with the children.

Play 'silhouette snap' using a picture and a silhouette of each object.

Shadows on the wall –
using an overhead projector

What you need:

▶ The projector needs to be at the correct height for the children to use it easily. Make sure that resources that the children can select are nearby and well organised.

▶ Images can be projected onto walls or pull down screens, or you could hang up a sheet.

▶ Provide a range of resources, natural and man made, translucent and opaque for the children to use.

> ▶ **Try to use an overhead projector which doesn't heat up (or switch itself off!) when left on for long periods – older models are often better.**
>
> ▶ **Find a safe place to set up the overhead projector – next to a wall socket so there are no trailing leads.**

Making connections

Overhead projectors can be used in many different ways to support investigation and exploration.
Children will really enjoy using an overhead projector as part of their daily activities.

Key words

light	shadow
mesh	sieve
screen	mirror
pattern	mosaic
overhead	projector

Talking and thinking:

▶ Talk to the children about how the overhead projector works. Place an object on the projector and watch what happens.

Ask: 'Where does the light come from?' 'How does the shadow appear on the wall?' Investigate how the projector works and observe how the mirror reflects light and shadow onto the wall.

Exploring:

▶ Encourage the children to investigate a wide range of objects and the shadows that they make.

▶ Give them time to discover what happens when different things are placed on the overhead projector screen. Try coins, buttons, cut out shapes, transparent sweet wrappers.

▶ Feathers and leaf skeletons, for example, will help the children develop close observation skills.

Documenting:

▶ The children may wish to record their findings through close observational drawing. Ensure there are good quality, fine drawing pencils and pens available close at hand.

▶ It is important to capture what the children say as they make their discoveries. Stand back and write down what they say.

More investigations

Using a set of mosaic shapes will enable pattern and picture making.

Investigate objects with holes – buttons, mesh, sieve, grater.

Ask: 'What happens when objects overlap?'

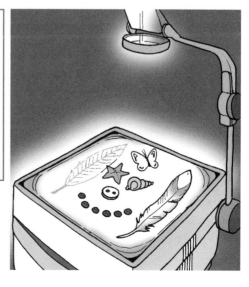

Imaginary worlds –
interacting with an overhead projector

What you need:

▶ Set up the overhead projector so that it projects across an area where the children can use large construction blocks.

▶ Put a screen behind where the children will build (you may need to block out some light to change the usual environment).

▶ Provide an interesting range of resources to use with the projector.

Encourage the children to add to these. You could include leaves, feathers, grasses, seed pods, shells and coloured acetate.

Resources should be well organised and available next to the projector.

> ▶ **Make sure that the projector is at an appropriate height for children to use safely and that all trailing leads are securely taped to the floor.**

Making connections

This investigation follows on from 'Shadows on the wall' (p42). It gives children the opportunity to bring together lots of different ideas – with very creative outcomes.

Key words

leaves	grasses
feathers	shell
high	low
under	shadow
build	project
seed pods	blocks

Talking and thinking:

▶ Talk with the children about how they will use the resources available to them to create imaginary worlds. This will involve sharing space, resources and ideas.

Ask: 'Where does the light come from?' 'How does the shadow appear on the wall?' Investigate how the projector works and observe how the mirror reflects light and shadow onto the wall.

Exploring:

Give the children time to investigate the different effects they can produce by:

▶ building and constructing;

▶ changing, and adding to, the materials on the projector;

▶ enacting stories while they build;

▶ introducing other equipment into the area.

Documenting:

▶ This activity will work best if the construction is left intact over a period of time. It will allow children to revisit and develop their creative ideas. Observe children over time to capture their achievements, interests and learning styles. Repeat the activity at a later date.

Ask: 'Do you remember when...?'

More investigations

Try adding music – let the children choose the music and operate the CD player or tape recorder independently as they work.

Use line drawings on acetate on the overhead projector to create a backdrop for the construction.

Make it bigger! –
making megabeasts

What you need:

In this activity the children will be using the overhead projector to create large versions of pictures and drawings they make – for displays, banners or wall hangings. Use drawings of minibeasts, flowers, seeds, shells or feathers, on acetate or tracing paper, or you could photocopy drawings onto acetate/OHP film.

▶ You need to decide how big you want the final images to be – choose an appropriate sized, light-coloured piece of paper.

▶ Fix this on the wall, at a height children can reach.

▶ Move the overhead projector so that the projected image is in the right place and is the size you have chosen.

▶ Use felt pens, crayons or paint to draw the outline of the projected image.

▶ **Take great care to tape the projector lead to the floor safely.**

Making connections

This investigation could follow on from 'Looking closely' (p26). The large scale displays will enhance any area of learning and provide many opportunities for mathematical and expressive language.

Key words

bigger	**smaller**
size	**outline**
display	**design**
crayon	**pastel**
projector	**banner**
pen	**edge**

Talking and thinking:

▶ This is an opportunity for individuals and groups of children to state preferences and make choices about which drawings they wish to use.

▶ Look at the drawings and discuss with the children which ones will be used to make the large picture.

Ask: 'Why have you chosen these drawings?' 'Why do you think they will work well?'

Exploring:

▶ Encourage the children to collaborate as they experiment with their drawings to discover which ones produce the clearest images.

▶ Provide a range of mark making resources – pens, pastels, crayons, and encourage the children to investigate where to stand to do this activity.

▶ As a group, decide how to complete the design you are making.

Documenting:

▶ This is an opportunity to involve the children in creating a striking display for their learning environment.

▶ Record their involvement in this process through photographs and comments. Display the original drawings alongside the finished megabeasts to show the children's involvement in the design process.

More investigations

Try projecting the images onto clear plastic. Use permanent markers to draw the outlines. The children can then paint in the detail as they choose, with PVA added to the paint. Display against a light source.

Project onto fabric to make interesting displays or curtains.

Looking through – using the overhead projector

What you need:

▶ This activity focuses on using the overhead projector to explore transparent and translucent resources.

▶ Provide a wide range of resources that you think light will pass through. You might include beads, buttons, counters, overhead connecting people, overhead mosaics and shapes. Encourage the children to add to this collection as they explore and investigate.

▶ Join in and model appropriate language. Children will enjoy using the correct technical terms.

> **Make sure the overhead projector and resources are safe and accessible for the children to use independently.** **!**

Making connections

You could use the overhead projector as an 'interest area' with a particular focus on one of the 6 areas of learning.

A day at the beach

Key words

bead	button
overhead	above
translucent	opaque
transparent	besides
connect	counter
ceiling	mosaic

Talking and thinking:

▶ Working with two or three children, investigate what happens when cellophane is placed on the projector.

▶ Look at the image on the wall or screen.

▶ Talk about the light passing through some objects and not others.

▶ Remind them about their discoveries with shadows.

Ask: 'Why do you think the image is coloured (or clear)?'

Exploring:

▶ Explore the effect of altering the position of the mirror to project on to different surfaces – the ceiling, the wall or a friend!

▶ Investigate patterns and shapes by putting objects on the overhead and projecting them on to the wall or screen.

▶ Explore the effects produced when one object is placed on top of another.

Documenting:

▶ Some of the images which are projected will be dramatic and worth capturing in photographs. These will demonstrate the children's creativity and imagination and their use of ICT. Talking to the children about the photographs will provide evidence of their scientific and mathematical understanding.

More investigations

In a small group, investigate mathematical problems using the overhead and connecting people, counters and shapes.

Look closely at the different effects produced by using 2-D and 3-D shapes.

Try small coloured bottles, bowls or tumblers.

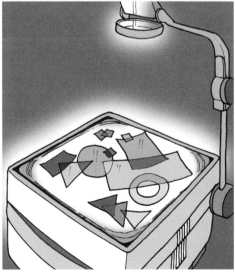

Shadow play – putting on a show

What you need:

I will need

▶ Use a ready made puppet theatre or make one from a large cardboard box (see 'The Little Book of Puppet Making' for ideas).

▶ Use muslin, voile or a fine sheet to create a screen at the front of the 'stage'.

▶ Set up a strong light (a clip-on spotlight or an anglepoise lamp) behind the performance area so that it shines onto the screen. The puppet theatre should be positioned so that the children can work the puppets from below without being seen.

▶ Provide a variety of strong paper, thin card, sticks, tape, string and fastenings for the children to use to make shadow puppets. A choice of tools should be accessible to the children at all times.

> **The light will get hot! Keep it safely out of children's reach.** !

Making connections

Revisit the children's earlier shadow investigations and ideas to recall which shapes will make good puppets. Inventing characters and making up stories about them will support children's language development.

Key words

screen	stage
puppet	theatre
spotlight	lamp
square	circle
shape	triangle
outline	shadow

Talking and thinking:

- Explore the puppet theatre and talk about screens, lights and shadows.
- Discuss a familiar story with the children and identify the main characters and the sequence of events.
- Talk about bringing the story to life using puppets and discuss how the puppet characters could be made. The children will need to negotiate which puppet or prop each of them will make.

Exploring:

- As the children draw their designs, encourage them to think about size, shape and outline. For some children you may want to provide 2-D shapes as templates to draw round.
- Help them to select the tools and techniques they need to shape, assemble and join the materials they are using.
- Try out the shadow puppets and prepare for the performance!

Documenting:

- Make a book called 'The Story of our Shadow Play' which can be shared with parents. You can include the designs for the puppets and any modifications that are made, as well as stories that the children narrate or write.
- Video the performance so that the puppeteers can see their own show.

More investigations

The children could:

- change the designs of their puppets to improve how they work
- make new characters or props for the story
- make up a new story for their characters.

A shade for Teddy

What you need:

▶ Collect together a range of different hats and other headgear. These might include a straw hat, a headscarf, a visor or peaked cap.

▶ You could also collect pictures of babies in sunhats and people wearing hats and using other objects to protect themselves from the sun. If possible, include in your collection some examples of parasols made of paper or fabric.

▶ Ask the children to bring a teddy from home.

▶ Provide a range of resources for making sun protectors for the teddies – paper, card, fabric, joining materials and fasteners – and a range of appropriate tools.

▶ Make these readily available and well organised to encourage children to make choices and develop independence as they experiment with making sun protection for their teddies.

If you choose a sunny day, the testing will be easier!

Making connections

This investigation links with topics on inside and outside; the clothes we wear; hot and cold; safe in the sun and what things are made of.

Key words

hat	visor
paper	fabric
shade	peak
cap	headscarf
card	cool
parasol	fasten/fix

Talking and thinking:

- Talk about why it is important to be protected from the sun.
- Look at a range of different hats and parasols and ask the children to make judgements about:
  - ▷ which they like best and why
  - ▷ who might wear them
  - ▷ which is best at keeping out the sun.
- Discuss the best way to keep Teddy safe from the sun when he goes out to play.

Exploring:

Ask the children to design a protective hat for Teddy. They may want to draw several pictures before choosing the one they want to make.

Remind them to think about the size of the hat, its shape, and how it will stay on. Using their designs, support the children as they make their hats.

Test them in the sun to see how well they keep Teddy in the shade.

Talk about how to improve the hats.

Documenting:

- Take photographs of the teddies wearing their hats.
- Display the hat and parasol collection alongside the photographs – you could set up a garden parasol indoors to make an exciting place for your display.
- Use the photos on another occasion to show the children how their skills and ideas have developed.

More investigations

Invite children, teddies, parents and carers to a Teddy Bears' Picnic – all wearing hats! Use this as activity to talk about keeping safe in the sun.

Investigate: What happens if the wind blows? Which teddy's hat stays on in the wind? Why?

Useful background knowledge

Light

Light is a form of radiation which is given out by a range of sources including the sun, electric and fluorescent light bulbs, fire and candles. Light travels in straight lines from its source in all directions. When it hits an object some of the light is absorbed and the rest bounces off from the surface of the object. When light bouncing from the surface of an object enters our eye, we then 'see' that object. We can sense light because our eyes contain nerve endings which, when stimulated by light entering the eye, transmit messages to the brain. These messages are translated in our brain to images that have shape, depth and colour – these are the objects we 'see'.

Transparent

A material which is transparent will allow almost all of the light falling on it to pass through it. An example is a sheet of clear glass. If you look through a transparent material you will be able to clearly see the shape, outline and colour of objects on the other side of it.

Opaque

A material which is opaque does not allow any light to pass through – it either reflects or absorbs all of the light which falls on it. If a bright light is shone on an opaque material it will cast a shadow on the surface behind it.

Translucent

A translucent material allows some light to pass through, but reflects or absorbs the rest. If you look through a translucent material you will be able to see the vague shape of an object behind it, but will not be able to make out any definite features. Greaseproof paper is a good example of a translucent material.

The moon and the stars

The moon is not a source of light. Instead, it reflects the light of the sun. The moon orbits around the earth and appears to change shape over the course of a month depending on where it is in its orbit. A full moon can be very bright, bright enough to cast pale shadows of opaque objects. The stars are sources of light and appear tiny because they are so far away. The sun is a star and appears larger to us on earth because it is closer than the other stars. Because the sun is so bright, we can only see the other stars at night. 'The sun is the brightest star in the sky'.

Songs, rhymes and poems

Nursery Rhymes

'Twinkle, Twinkle Little Star'
'Star Light, Star Bright'
'Girls and Boys Come out to Play'
'I See the Moon and the Moon Sees Me'
'The Sun Has Got His Hat On'

Bed in Summer

R.L.Stevenson

In winter I get up at night
And dress by yellow candle light.
In summer, quite the other way,
I have to go to bed by day.

My Shadow

R.L.Stevenson

I have a little shadow that goes in and out with me
And what can be the use of him is more than I can see.
He is very, very like me from the heels up to the head;
And I see him jump before me when I jump into my bed.
The funniest thing about him is the way he likes to grow –
Not at all like proper children, which is always very slow;
For he sometimes shoots up taller like an India-rubber ball,
And he sometimes gets so little that there's none of him at all.

Resources

Design and Making Centre
Church Road
Pool Redruth
Cornwall TR15 3PZ
01209 719 354

Suppliers of:

▶ Tools for making shadow puppets, fasteners, joining materials.

▶ Rectangular 4.5 volt batteries with brass strip connectors.

Reflections on Learning
Arkwright Road
Bicester
Oxfordshire OX26 4UU
01869 366 166

www.reflectionsonlearning.co.uk

Suppliers of:

▶ Light boxes and light stations.

▶ Resources for use on overhead projectors and light boxes.

Commotion Group
Commotion House
Morely Road
Tonbridge
Kent TN9 1RA
01732 773 399

www.commotiongroup.co.uk

Suppliers of:

▶ Electrical components – bulbs, leads with crocodile clips, bulb holders.

▶ Torches, magnifiers, viewers, binoculars and telescopes.

▶ Translucent materials for use on an overhead projector – connecting people, mosaic shapes, plastic counters, coloured acetate, colour paddles.

▶ Overhead projector screens.

More information:

Department for Communities and Local Government
www.gov.uk/firekills

Suppliers of:

▶ Fire safety leaflets and video.

London Fire Brigade
www.london-fire.gov.uk

Suppliers of:

▶ An advice leaflet for parents about the dangers of children playing with or setting fires, and also teaching resources related to fire safety.